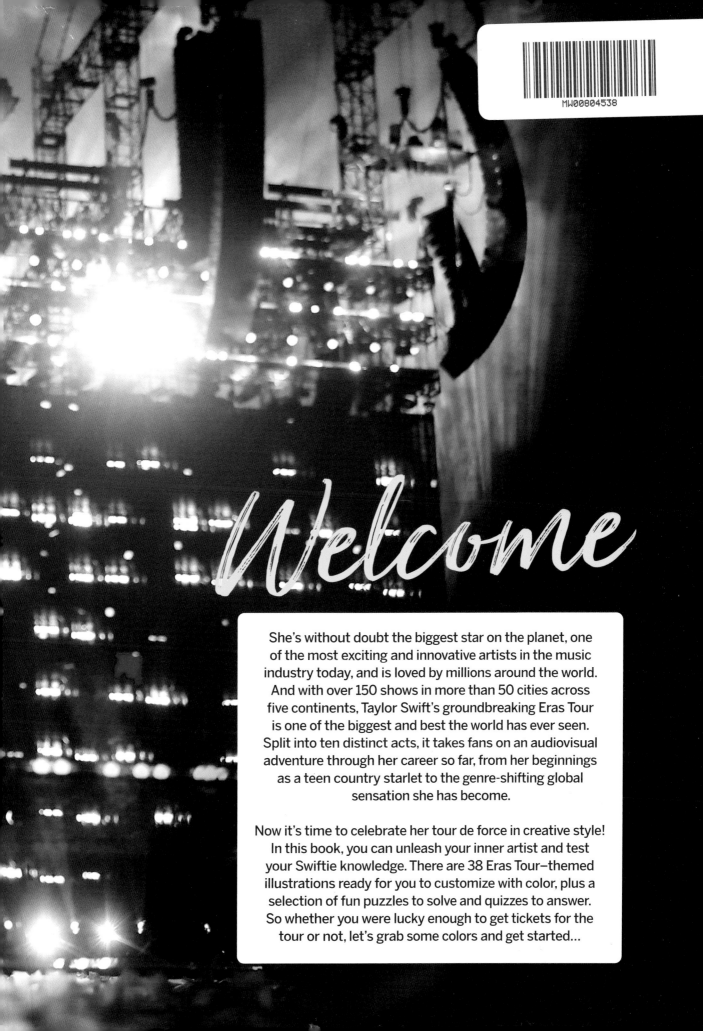

Welcome

She's without doubt the biggest star on the planet, one of the most exciting and innovative artists in the music industry today, and is loved by millions around the world. And with over 150 shows in more than 50 cities across five continents, Taylor Swift's groundbreaking Eras Tour is one of the biggest and best the world has ever seen. Split into ten distinct acts, it takes fans on an audiovisual adventure through her career so far, from her beginnings as a teen country starlet to the genre-shifting global sensation she has become.

Now it's time to celebrate her tour de force in creative style! In this book, you can unleash your inner artist and test your Swiftie knowledge. There are 38 Eras Tour–themed illustrations ready for you to customize with color, plus a selection of fun puzzles to solve and quizzes to answer. So whether you were lucky enough to get tickets for the tour or not, let's grab some colors and get started…

Contents

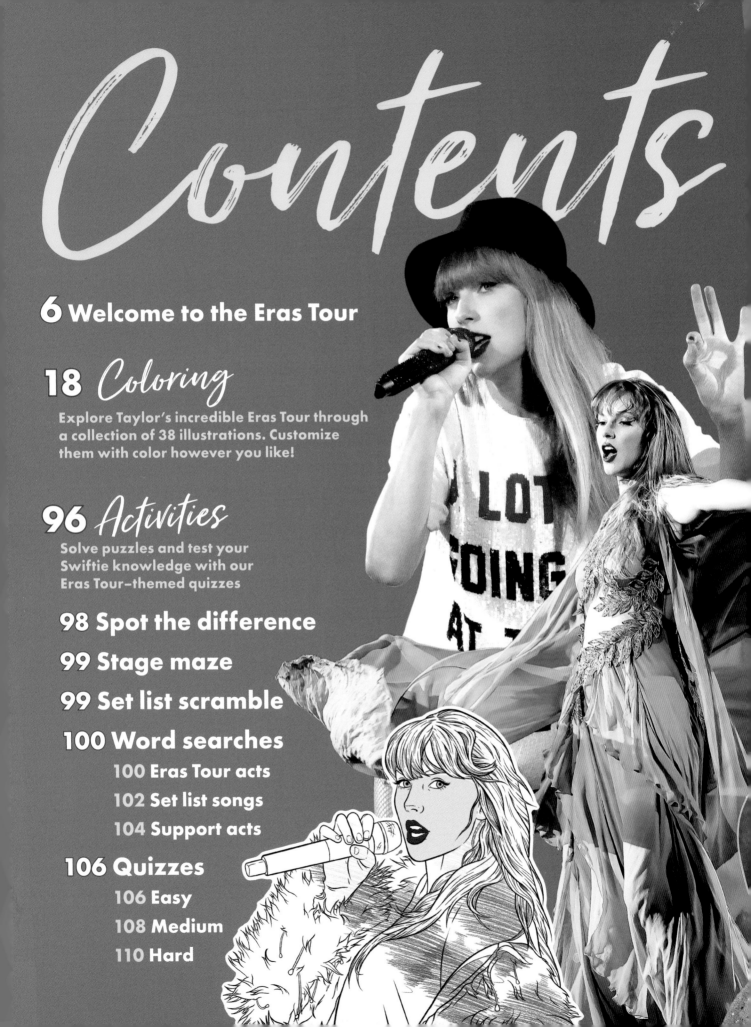

Taylor kicks things off with *Lover* before taking fans on a journey through her musical eras.

Welcome
···· to the ····
Eras Tour

The groundbreaking world tour has been an unrivaled cultural triumph, journeying through the legendary career of Taylor Swift across two years and more than 150 shows.

Are you ready for it? It had been five long years since Taylor went on tour, so anticipation was high. She made the announcement in November 2022 on *Good Morning America*, confirming the tour name and that it would in fact cover all of her "eras" as a musical journey through her full back catalog.

And what a catalog. She had stayed very busy since her last tour (Reputation World Tour, ending in 2018), releasing new albums (*Lover*, *folklore*, *evermore*, and *Midnights*) and embarking on her mammoth journey to re-record her first six albums, releasing *Fearless (Taylor's Version)* and *Red (Taylor's Version)* as faithful replicas of the originals, alongside unheard new material "from the Vault." Fans and the media alike were baffled as to how she could possibly fit this 17-year-long career, studded with smash hits and iconic moments, fan favorites and a broad range of genres, into a standard hour-and-a-half show. They'd soon find out it was no standard show at all…

The battle for tickets
Before they could learn how she'd possibly squeeze every era into one live performance, Swifties had to secure their seats in the stadiums. What followed was an unprecedented ticket-buying frenzy that landed entertainment giant Ticketmaster in a congressional hearing. The demand was so extraordinarily high that tickets actually sold out before the general sale even began. Ticketmaster said there were 14 million people attempting to buy 600,000 tickets, meaning Taylor would have to perform around 900 shows to meet demand.

For the lucky fans who had secured their spot on the tour, Taylor was hard at work preparing the show. She later told *TIME* magazine in her "Person of the Year" interview that she rehearsed by singing the entire show on a treadmill every day.

The Eras Tour kicks off
The Eras Tour began in March 2023. The scale of the tour is truly astronomical: over 150 dates, covering 17 years and 11 albums, generating $1 billion gross sales in the United States alone. It tracks, then, that the set list itself is mammoth in size.

Swifties show off their friendship bracelets in Rio de Janeiro, Brazil.

Taylor making dreams come true for one lucky fan during her show in São Paulo, Brazil.

All eyes were on Glendale, Arizona, to witness the opening performance of the Eras Tour. It was there at State Farm Stadium that fans were delighted to discover the show was almost twice the expected length, jam-packed with hits and deep cuts.

Taylor covers 11 eras across each three-hour show. Each "era" corresponds to an album and a time in Taylor's life, and is highlighted in a distinct section of the concert. This journey through her music reminds us of how many hits, genres, and aesthetics Taylor has had over her career. Within one show we are high-kicking in sequined slogan tees, and just moments later we're lost in a mystical woods being guided by a witches' coven. The variety of the show is testament to Taylor's versatility, something she highlights each night with a rotating set list of acoustic tracks. Each show includes two surprise songs, giving Taylor the chance to perform as many of her songs from across her canon as she wishes.

The ambition of the show stretches beyond the mammoth-length set list, too: each era is fully produced, complete with intricate choreography (like the musical-themed "Vigilante Shit"), stunning audiovisual effects (as in the gasp-inducing "Bad Blood" pyrotechnics), and a closet befitting the world's biggest pop star. The fashion of the Eras Tour has been applauded for being her most stylish and fashion-forward yet. Indeed, Taylor's "tour-drobe" includes high-luxury pieces from the likes of Louboutin (the red-bottomed boots during the *Lover* era), Roberto Cavalli (the mismatching *1989* era two-pieces), Elie Saab (the enchanting gown for "Enchanted" performances), and

Vivienne Westwood (the torn wedding dress–inspired gown for the *Tortured Poets Department* era). Fans have been so smitten with her outfits on stage, hundreds of Swifties tune in to live streams each night to predict every look across up to 16 costume changes, and many have re-created the costumes for their own Eras Tour outfits.

The set lists

As of May 2024, a month after Taylor dropped the double album *The Tortured Poets Department*, the Eras Tour squeezed an incredible ten acts—or eras—into a three-hour extravaganza performance.

Taylor picks up her live performances where she left off: with *Lover*. This was Swift's first self-owned album, and was the last album she released before her touring hiatus. Indeed, "Lover Fest," the festival Taylor had planned to mark her seventh studio album, had to be called off due to the 2020 pandemic. After emerging from tie-dyed giant butterfly "wings," Taylor launches into the album's hits. This era is bedazzled, filled with empowering tracks and glittering silver and pink outfits. It also contains one of the tour's most impactful moments: when Taylor invites the crowd to join her in "crossing the first bridge" of the evening: "Cruel Summer" launches the show proper. The song's rekindled fame relaunched it onto the charts, where it reached number one on the *Billboard* charts an impressive four years after its release. Now that's what you call a "sleeper hit"!

From the *Lover* set, we rewind back a decade, to 2008's *Fearless* era. Fueled by nostalgia, the crowds delight in some of Taylor's earliest smash hits: the hopelessly romantic

"THE AMBITION OF THE SHOW STRETCHES BEYOND THE MAMMOTH SET LIST"

Taylor has worn over 60 stunning outfits and dresses during the Eras Tour.

"THE CROWDS SCREAMING THE BRIDGE OF 'ALL TOO WELL' IS A HIGHLIGHT"

"Fearless," the Romeo and Juliet retelling "Love Story," and the pop masterclass "You Belong with Me." This trio of songs certainly pack a punch. It's one of Swifties' most beloved albums: it earned Taylor her first Grammy, marked her early breakout from the country genre, and includes iconic Swiftian imagery of high school, fairy tales, and, of course, dancing in the rain. This set is rife with nostalgic moments, from Taylor's dazzling dresses, the heart-hands being held aloft during "Fearless," and naturally, the bejeweled cowboy boots.

Next up is *Red*. This set includes a heartwarming moment between Taylor and a chosen fan each night, when the Swiftie is invited to the end of the stage for a hug and is gifted Taylor's signed hat. Taylor's costumes during the *Red* era includes another "22" music video reference: her T-shirt is emblazoned with lyrics or phrases like "This is not Taylor's Version" in homage to the video's iconic look. She rounds out the *Red* era with a full-length acoustic guitar performance of "All Too Well (Ten Minute Version)"—the crowds screaming the bridge is certainly a highlight of the evening. This song is among the most legendary from across Taylor's archives: it began as a beloved "track five," with rumors of a longer version swirling around online for years before Taylor finally conceded a release of the longer cut in the *Red (Taylor's Version)* Vault tracks. The song became the longest-length track to hit number one on the charts, and its accompanying short film music video won multiple awards.

Taylor makes a quick pit stop by the *Speak Now* era with "Enchanted," dazzling in a sumptuous ball gown to complete the fairy-tale feel. She briefly added fan favorite "Long Live" to this section in honor of the release of *Speak Now (Taylor's Version)*, which she announced on stage in Nashville.

From here, we rocket into the *reputation* era. It's quite the contrast from the wondrous fairy tale of *Speak Now*, complete with thunderous drums, fire show, and epic snake visuals. Taylor has consistently worn a black bodysuit with a slithering red snake across it for every show, a detail fans interpreted as a statement on her actual reputation: despite it all, it never changes. This set features the rock-gospel power ballad "Don't Blame Me," and an Easter egg–filled "Look What You Made Me Do" sees multiple "Taylors" trapped behind glass, vying to escape, symbolizing her well-publicized efforts to retake ownership of her music.

From the fiery fury of *reputation*, we head into calmer territory—*folklore* and *evermore* share a chapter in the Eras Tour ever since the introduction of *The Tortured Poets Department* chapter later in the show. The combined albums (Taylor describes them as "sisters," having written and released them so close together) are set in an abandoned woodland cabin with ethereal gowns and even witch cloaks for costumes. Here, Taylor sings the "teenage love triangle" trio of songs: "betty," "cardigan," and "august," telling the interweaving story of *folklore*'s fictional romance. This chapter of the tour also contains a new fan tradition: a standing ovation lasting several minutes after every performance of "champagne problems."

The *1989* era is a tour of Taylor's breakout album. It's this era that cemented her pop legend status, and its set list includes some of her biggest smash hits and fan favorites. It's a nonstop dance chapter, with fans dancing so passionately they have caused multiple "Swift Quakes"—mini earthquakes—during "Shake It Off." This chapter of the show is a thrilling retelling of Taylor's pure-pop glory days, and set the scene perfectly for the announcement of *1989 (Taylor's Version)* in Los Angeles.

Taylor released *The Tortured Poets Department* in April 2024 while on a tour break before relaunching with the European leg. The introduction of this album to the Eras Tour meant a rejigging of the other chapters to make room for her latest work to shine. It's a melodramatic and moody snapshot of the 31-song album, with powerful vocals and bewitching visuals: Taylor lovingly called the set "Feminine Rage: The Musical." This chapter almost acts as a short play, with Taylor's character beginning the scene rebelliously in love, before being abandoned and scorned, then turning her scorn outward at a witch trial. Her character, despite her exhaustion and heartbreak, is propped up in time for her final act: the meta performance of "I Can Do It with a Broken Heart," a song about the Eras Tour.

Next up follows the most varied section of the evening: the acoustic set. Each night, Taylor chooses a song to perform on acoustic guitar, and then another on piano. It's an intimate part of the show that highlights her songwriting skills: every song she has in her archives can be stripped back to this simple format and still shine. When she began the tour, these surprise songs were limited to a one-time performance. She rewrote this self-imposed rule while in Australia, saying she no longer wanted to limit herself. She's also used this section to draw narrative connections from across her catalog: creating mashups with thematically similar songs (such as the "murder mash up" of "Carolina" and "no body, no crime") or to complete the story of one song with another (for example, "The Great War" with "You're Losing Me").

The acoustic set has been host to announcements: this is where she has announced new re-recorded albums, music videos, and special editions of new albums. It's also been where she hosts special guests. Support acts Sabrina Carpenter and Gracie Abrams have both joined her for a duet in the acoustic set, as have collaborators Jack Antonoff, Maren Morris, and Marcus Mumford. Longtime producer Aaron Dessner appeared at multiple shows to play fan favorites alongside Taylor, including "ivy" and "The Great War."

Each show is closed out with a tour of the *Midnights* era. The final chapter glitters as Taylor moves through some of her biggest hits to date: waving to the crowds during "Anti-Hero" and emerging from umbrellas in a sequined bodysuit for "Midnight Rain." This set features a memorably sultry performance of revenge song "Vigilante Shit," infused with Broadway's *Chicago*-style choreography. She ends with the celebratory, joyous "Karma" (occasionally joined by collaborator Ice Spice, occasionally shouting out

The show lasts over three hours and ends with the *Midnights* set.

"THE *1989* ERA IS A TOUR OF TAYLOR'S BREAKOUT ALBUM"

Fun Fact

Ticketmaster estimated 31 million people registered for pre-sale in Canada—that's 75% of their population!

"THE JOYOUS ATMOSPHERE HAS BEEN A CELEBRATION OF FEMININITY IN ALL ITS FORMS"

boyfriend Travis Kelce with the amended lyric "Karma is the guy on the Chiefs, coming straight home to me"). It's a truly bombastic and joyous way to close out the show, leaving the crowds shimmering with energy as the finale confetti falls to the ground.

The year of the Swiftie

Taylor fans have been having a blast at the Eras Tour. The fan traditions have piled up: from chanting the countdown "one, two, three, let's go bitch!" to holding minutes-long standing ovations. Outfits are carefully curated, often months in advance, taking inspiration from across the Swift world. Fans have decked themselves out in stitch-perfect replicas of Taylor's outfits from tours and music videos, or in interpretations of her lyrics (fans have been spotted in inventive costumes such as a lime-green dog in reference to "the last great american dynasty," and even as the traffic lights from "Death by a Thousand Cuts").

The most enduring, and charming, is of course the tradition of friendship bracelets. This trend began organically, inspired by the song "You're on Your Own, Kid," in which Taylor encourages us to live life wholeheartedly ("so make the friendship bracelets, take the moment and taste it"). Before the tour began, hardcore Swifties planned friendship bracelet exchanges as direct fan-to-fan exchanges, but it proved so popular and so life-affirming that it spiraled beyond individual fans and became a crowd-wide, tour-wide phenomenon.

The inclusive, joyous atmosphere has been a real celebration of nostalgia and femininity in all its forms. Cultural commentators have noted that the Eras Tour, compounded by the blockbuster release of *Barbie* and a litany of hyper-feminine trends, has had the effect of "reclaiming girlhood," in particular during the summer of 2023 at the height of the tour's U.S. leg. The shared experience of the Eras Tour is one rooted in the full spectrum of self-expression the show encourages: the thrill of dancing to "Shake It Off" lined up next to the catharsis of singing "champagne problems."

If this were a movie...

Outside of the stadium walls, Swifties found new and inventive ways to enjoy the tour. Fans were tailgating (or "Taygating") in the concert perimeter, and tuning in to livestreams en masse each night to experience the tour without a ticket. Then along came the official concert film. *The Eras Tour* film followed a similar trajectory as the concert itself, breaking records and becoming a cultural force in its own right.

Filmed over several shows in Los Angeles, the film was directed by the award-winning Sam Wrench, the mind behind concert documentaries for Billie Eilish and BTS. After being given special dispensation to make the film during the SAG-AFTRA strikes of 2023 (thanks to Taylor's commitment to the unions of fair conditions for everyone involved), it took hundreds of cameras and microphones to transform multiple live performances into one seamless movie.

The show was updated in 2024 to include songs from *The Tortured Poets Department*.

The film was a runaway success, becoming the highest-grossing concert film of all time. This is in part thanks to Taylor's unusual decision to "cut out the middleman" and distribute the movie directly to theaters, bypassing traditional studios. It's also in large part due to her encouragement to fans to enjoy themselves in the theaters as though it were a live concert. Swifties were seen dancing in the aisles of sold-out movie theaters, often dressed in full Taylor-inspired costumes. Even Taylor herself was swept up in the excitement: she was spotted dancing and joining in with fan chants at the film's premiere in Los Angeles.

The Eras Tour film was an astounding commercial success, earning over $260 million to become the highest-grossing concert film of all time (tickets were $19.89, of course!). It was also a critical success, and earned an unprecedented Golden Globe nomination for Cinematic and Box Office Achievement. It soon rolled out to streaming, with Disney+ scoring the rights and Swifties worldwide hosting viewing parties.

The billion-dollar tour

The Eras Tour has been an incredible commercial feat. It is the highest-grossing tour of all time, surpassing Elton John's Farewell Yellow Brick Road Tour, and was the first (and to date, only) tour to reach $1 billion in gross revenue. Taylor herself is estimated to have made $500 million from the show, an impressive paycheck that tipped her into officially becoming a billionaire. She's the only billionaire to date to have reached this rarefied status through her music alone (other giants like Jay-Z and Rihanna reached this point thanks to a combination of their other ventures). The show is projected to hit $2 billion in gross revenue by the time of the final curtain call in December 2024.

And it's not just Taylor making money from the show. She has made generous donations to local charities and food banks at each stop of the tour, and provided an unbelievable $55 million in bonuses to her U.S. tour team. This included the now-famous move of giving every one of the show's truck drivers a $100,000 bonus: changing the

"THE ERAS TOUR HAS PROPELLED FANDOM CULTURE TO NEW LEVELS"

lives of the people who help overcome the Eras Tour's impressive logistical challenges every night.

The world is in its Swiftie era

Taylor has taken the world by storm: the Eras Tour's cultural impact has been epic. The devotion and passion she invokes from fans has been dubbed "Taylormania" or "Swiftmania," the likes of which have not been seen since the height of Beatlemania in the 1960s. Fanaticism for artists is nothing new, but the Eras Tour has propelled fandom culture to new levels of enthusiasm and scale. Indeed, the Eras Tour's impact was felt well beyond the stadiums, and we're not just talking about the "Shake It Off"-induced earthquakes. Cities rename themselves, host Swift-themed parties, exhibitions, and events, and shower Taylor with keys to the city. Even Rio's iconic modern wonder of the world—Christ the Redeemer—was seen sporting a "Junior Jewels" T-shirt (a reference to the iconic "You Belong with Me" music video pajamas).

Perhaps the enthusiasm from her host cities is down to the sizable economic impact of the Eras Tour. This phenomenon has been coined "the Swift Lift" by economists. Wherever the tour visits benefits from a financial boom, thanks to Taylor's fans spending at hotels, on travel, on outfits and merchandise, and in restaurants and bars. The tour is credited with helping the recovering entertainment and tourist industries from a post-pandemic slump, and was even name-checked by the U.S. Federal Reserve as a key contributor to the year's economy. It's no surprise then that countries have been falling over themselves to lay out the red carpet for Taylor. Singapore even went as far as brokering a controversial deal with her team to guarantee exclusivity to Singapore in their region, and it took Prime Minister Justin Trudeau writing a public letter to Taylor to convince her to put Canadian dates on her to-do list.

The Eras Tour legacy

This tour has been historic by any measure. From the initial ticket sale chaos through to the final performance, the Eras Tour has been an unrivaled commercial success and an unparalleled cultural force. It has forever cemented Taylor as a legend, a singular tour de force and a legacy artist. She confirmed at her 100th show in Liverpool, U.K., that the tour would end after its 152nd date in Vancouver in December 2024. She said: "This has definitely been exhausting, all-encompassing, but [the] most joyful, most rewarding, most wonderful thing that has ever happened in my life, this tour…" And while she absolutely deserves a well-earned rest after more than 450 hours on the stage, performing across 20 countries and two years, if we know anything about Taylor Swift, it's that there's nothing she loves more than creating art for us to enjoy. While she's recharging, we will hold on to the memories of this groundbreaking tour, and these memories will hold on to us.

Travis Kelce (right) makes a surprise appearance in London.

Each show features two surprise acoustic songs from Taylor's archives.

Did You Know?

Taylor went viral for defending a fan mid-performance of "Bad Blood" from an over-eager security guard.

Coloring

Check off the ones you've done!

21

23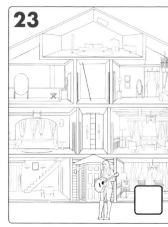

27

29

33

35

37

39

41

45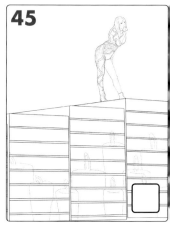

47

49

51

53

The Eras Tour is born

After teasing an upcoming tour while promoting her tenth album, *Midnights*, Taylor finally gave us the news we'd all been waiting for. She officially announced her Eras Tour on November 1, 2022, during an appearance on the TV show *Good Morning America* and via social media.

A musical journey

The Eras Tour would be Taylor's sixth concert tour and her biggest to date. Split into ten unique acts, with each celebrating a different "musical era" from Taylor's incredible career, the shows would feature a host of stunning outfits, amazing set designs, and some of the singer's biggest hits.

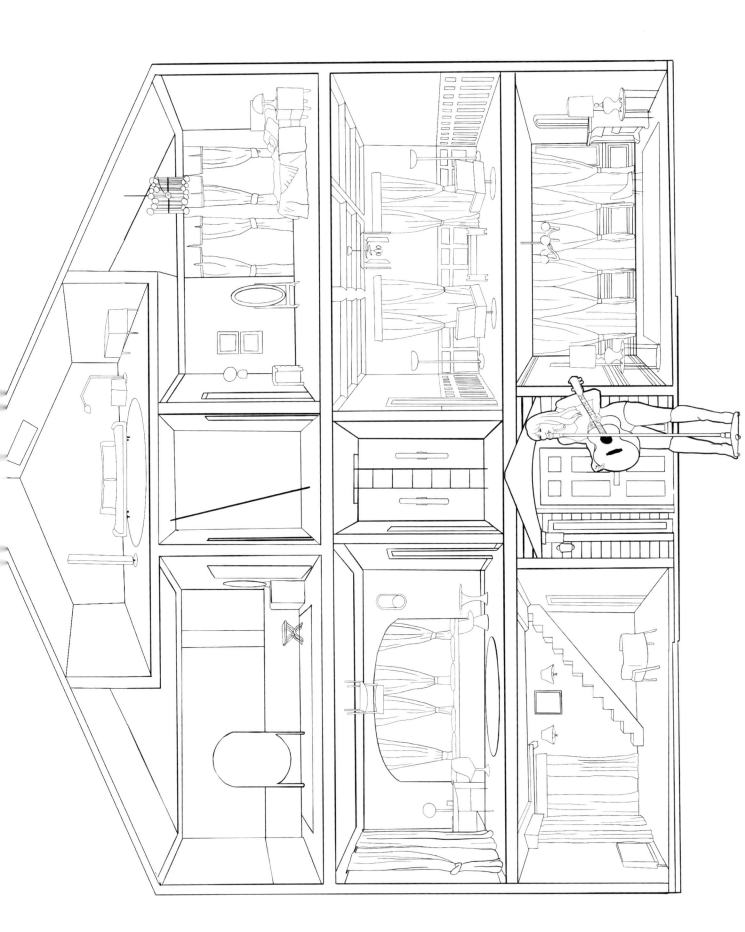

Tour fever

The demand for tickets was unprecedented, with Swifties around the world desperate to get a glimpse of their idol. In the United States, more than 2.4 million tickets were sold in the presale alone—the highest by an artist in a single day.

The Lover era

The Eras Tour kicked off in style in Glendale, Arizona, on March 17, 2023. The show opens with the *Lover* era, where Taylor runs through some of her hits from her seventh album, including "Cruel Summer" and "You Need to Calm Down." She dons her iconic *Lover* bodysuit, pairing it with a sparkly blazer during "The Man."

The Fearless era

Fearless comes next, with Taylor wowing fans with her stunning outfits—shimmering metallic flapper-style dresses in gold, silver, and black. Taylor's parents even helped her re-create the iconic *Fearless* guitar especially for the Eras Tour, decorating it with rhinestones the day before the opening show!

Dress to impress

Not only is Taylor the queen of pop, she's also an undisputed style icon. She's worn more than 60 different outfits during the Eras Tour—from bodysuits to ball gowns—and has changed outfits up to an incredible 16 times a night! For the European leg of the tour she even gave her wardrobe a refresh, introducing a host of new colors and styles.

Breaking through

It was her second album, *Fearless*, released in 2008, that brought Taylor to mainstream attention for the first time. Three of her hit singles from the Grammy Award–winning album feature in the Eras Tour set list: "You Belong with Me," "Love Story," and the album's title track.

The evermore era

For U.S. fans, the *evermore* era is up next, with the sequins and sparkle of *Fearless* replaced by moody, wintery woods and trees that seemingly grow out of the stage. For the European leg, Taylor merged *evermore* and *folklore*, creating "folkmore," to make space for *The Tortured Poets Department*.

A Swift surprise

Taylor stunned fans in December 2020 with the release of *evermore*, her ninth studio album, which came just five months after sister album *folklore*. Five songs from the indie folk record featured in the original set list, including U.S. #1 single "willow," "tolerate it," " 'tis the damn season," and "marjorie."

Mellow yellow

Sticking with the woodland theme, Taylor takes center stage on a moss-covered piano to perform "champagne problems." Murder-mystery tale "no body, no crime" would make an appearance in place of " 'tis the damn season" during shows in Los Angeles, Seattle, and Santa Clara as rock trio HAIM joined Taylor on the stage.

The reputation era

The glitz and glamour return with the *reputation* era. Taylor takes to the stage in her one and only *reputation* outfit. Designed by Roberto Cavalli, the iconic black one-legged jumpsuit features a bejeweled red snake design that winds from Taylor's leg all the way up to her neck.

Serpent symbolism

From Taylor's outfit to the set design, you may be wondering what's with all the snakes during the *reputation* chapter of the Eras Tour. Well, it all stems from a very public fallout between our favorite singer and Kim Kardashian in 2016, in which Kardashian appeared to refer to Taylor as a snake on social media.

Top of the pops

Released in November 2017, *reputation* was Taylor's sixth studio album and her fourth consecutive album to sell one million first-week copies in the United States. It also topped charts worldwide. Four songs from the album feature on the Eras Tour set list, including "...Ready for It?," "Delicate," and "Don't Blame Me."

I ♥ T.S.

Unsurprisingly, "Look What You Made Me Do," *reputation*'s lead single, also makes an appearance. In a nod to the song's iconic music video, Taylor's backup dancers perform in doll boxes dressed in outfits inspired by past versions of Taylor.

The Speak Now era

Next up, we're introduced to Taylor's third studio album. Released in October 2010, *Speak Now* charts our favorite singer's growth from adolescence to adulthood. It was written entirely by Taylor during her Fearless Tour and spent six weeks at #1 on the U.S. *Billboard* 200 charts.

Evolving eras

With Taylor's standard set list originally consisting of 44 of her best-loved songs, each Eras Tour show lasts over three hours! However, some *Speak Now* fans were left disappointed that only one song from the album—"Enchanted"—featured. Always one to keep her Swifties happy, Taylor added fan-favorite "Long Live" following the release of *Speak Now (Taylor's Version)* in July 2023.

Queen of pop

Big, beautiful ball gowns are the order of the day for the *Speak Now* era. Performing against a striking purple backdrop, Taylor looks like royalty in stunning gold, silver, blue, and baby pink dresses as she treats fans to "Enchanted" and "Long Live."

The Red era

Taylor kicks the *Red* era off with "22" from her fourth studio album. She also runs through the 2012 album's lead single "We Are Never Ever Getting Back Together" and "I Knew You Were Trouble." To the delight of Swifties everywhere, the fabled 10-minute version of "All Too Well" from the *Red* re-release brings the era to an emotional close.

One big family

In an effort to make Swifties feel even more connected to her Eras Tour shows, fans were given light-up wristbands that flash, pulse, and create patterns. Highlighting the positive community vibes, fans have even been making friendship bracelets for each other.

Girl in red

In a nod to an outfit she wore in the "22" music video, Taylor rocks a series of T-shirts with sequined slogans—including a twist on the iconic original with "A Lot Going On At The Moment" and "Who's Taylor Swift Anyway? Ew." Beneath the shirts is a stunning red-to-black bodysuit, which she complements with a sparkly red jacket during "All Too Well" and when she performed "Nothing New" with Phoebe Bridgers.

The folklore era

Released during the pandemic in July 2020, *folklore* was the first of Taylor's surprise indie-folk sister albums and her eighth studio album. The *folklore* act sees the return of Taylor's idyllic moss-covered forest cabin that we first saw during the 2021 Grammy Awards.

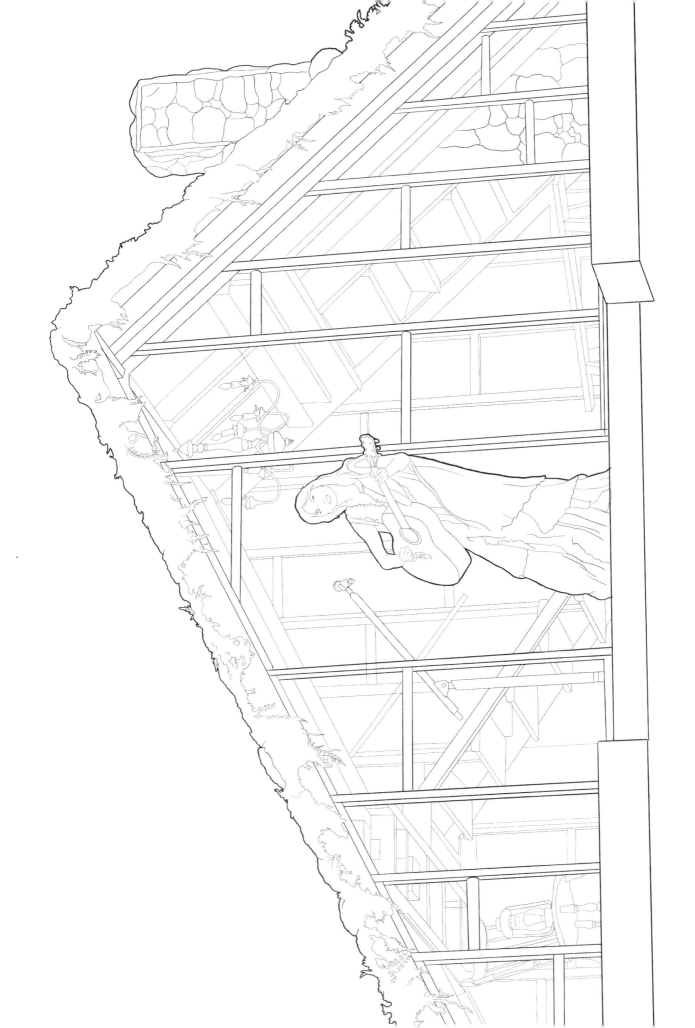

Cottagecore chic

The *folklore* act is all about floaty, textured dresses in a host of muted, natural colors. From Italian dressmaker Alberta Ferretti, Taylor has worn a number of dreamy designs in green, purple, cream, and more, which perfectly capture the ethereal aesthetic of this era.

Easter eggs

Swifties have been on the hunt for Taylor's Easter eggs ever since the tour kicked off and they went into a frenzy when, during a performance of "Bejeweled" from *Midnights*, she included moves from a fan's viral TikTok dance. Who says Taylor doesn't pay attention to her fans?!

Cabin fever

With the creation of "folkmore" for the Eras Tour's European leg, fans had to wave goodbye to *folklore*'s "the 1" and "the last great american dynasty." However, Taylor still treated them to a host of indie-folk hits, including "cardigan" atop her cabin, as well as "betty," "august," "illicit affairs," and "my tears ricochet."

The 1989 era

Considered by many fans and critics to be the best of Taylor's albums to date, *1989* was released in October 2014 and cemented her status as one of pop's biggest superstars. It features some of her biggest and best-loved hits and won Album of the Year and Best Pop Vocal Album at the 2016 Grammy Awards.

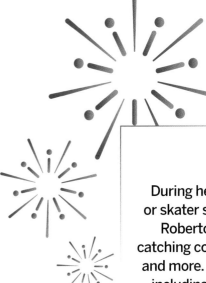

Retro revival

During her *1989* era, Taylor rocks a sparkly two-piece or skater skirt and crop top combo, both from designer Roberto Cavalli. The outfits come in a host of eye-catching colors, from orange and bright green to hot pink and more. She performs five of her hits from the album, including "Style," "Bad Blood," and "Wildest Dreams."

Taylor's versions

On August 9, 2023, during her show in Inglewood, California, Taylor announced *1989 (Taylor's Version)*, the latest of her re-recorded albums. It followed re-released versions of *Fearless*, *Red*, and *Speak Now*. Taylor also used her shows to premiere videos for "Karma" and "I Can See You."

Shake it up

Excitable Swifties literally made the earth move during the star's shows in Seattle in July 2023, causing seismic activity equal to a 2.3 magnitude earthquake. Fittingly, it's thought that it was during *1989*'s "Shake It Off," as well as "Blank Space," that the "Swift Quake" was created.

Surprise songs

To ensure no two Eras Tour shows are the same, Taylor includes an acoustic set featuring two surprise songs—one on the piano and one on guitar. Taylor's original plan was to play different surprise songs each night and only to repeat a song if she was unhappy with a previous version.

Taylor's friends

Throughout the Eras Tour, Taylor has been joined on stage by a number of special guests and supporting acts, from Paramore and Gayle, who opened the very first show of the tour, to Sabrina Carpenter, Phoebe Bridgers, HAIM, and more. To the delight of fans, Taylor even brought her boyfriend Travis Kelce on stage during a show in London!

Coming clean

Taylor repeated a surprise song—"Clean" from *1989*—for the first time during a show in East Rutherford in May 2023 after admitting she should have performed it in a higher key the first time around. During her final performance of 2023, she announced that she would be opening up all of her surprise songs once again for her 2024 dates.

The Midnights era

Sadly, all good things have to come to an end, and Taylor brings her Eras Tour show to a close in style with the *Midnights* act. She kicks off with the dreamy "Lavender Haze" before taking fans on a journey through her tenth album, performing the likes of "Anti-Hero" and "Midnight Rain" and ending with "Karma."

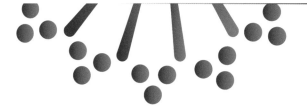

Going out in style

Taylor's outfits during the closing *Midnights* chapter are some of the most stunning of the entire show. One of the highlights is a fringed bodysuit from designer Oscar de la Renta that was hand-embroidered with over 5,300 crystals and beads, and which took an incredible 315 hours to make!

Record breaking

By the time the Eras Tour comes to an end in Vancouver in December 2024, Taylor will have performed more than 150 shows in over 50 cities across five continents. In December 2023, the tour became the highest-grossing in history after generating an incredible $1 billion in revenue.

The Eras Tour Movie

On October 13, 2023, the film *Taylor Swift: The Eras Tour* was released worldwide. Directed by Sam Wrench, the movie gave Swifties who weren't fortunate enough to get tickets the opportunity to experience the tour in all its glory. It earned over $260 million worldwide at the box office.

A new era

In February 2024, while accepting her 13th Grammy Award for Best Pop Vocal Album for *Midnights*, Taylor sent Swifties into overdrive as she announced her latest album, *The Tortured Poets Department*!

The TTPD era

Taylor's 11th studio album dropped on April 19, 2024, breaking a bunch of sales and streaming records in the process, as well as topping charts around the globe. As ever, Taylor had a surprise for Swifties up her sleeve—just two hours after the release, it was expanded into a 31-track double album!

Poetry in motion

Following the release of *TTPD*, Taylor revamped her set list ahead of the European leg of the Eras Tour. She added a host of new songs from the album, including lead single "Fortnight," while also showing off some stunning new outfits, such as the immediately iconic white Vivienne Westwood dress.

Activities

✓

Check off the ones you've done!

Spot the difference

Can you find the SIX changes made to the image on the bottom?

Solution on page 112

Get Taylor to the stage!

Help Taylor sneak past the fans to appear on the stage

Solution on page 112

Set list scramble

Unscramble these friendship bracelets to reveal songs from the Eras Tour set list

A L E C D E T I
1. _____

A M A R K
2. _____

E R O L V
3. _____

G D A A R C I N
4. _____

N E H A M T
5. _____

D C E N T E H N A
6. _____

Word search

Can you find these 10 Eras Tour acts
(plus one Easter egg!) in the puzzle?

```
D  S  R  O  U  T  T  K  E  I  T  W  E  V  Y
D  E  K  D  O  O  E  R  A  S  M  O  V  I  E
B  S  R  P  H  U  O  T  E  E  T  N  Q  A  P
Z  X  D  L  R  L  W  X  E  V  V  W  G  E  N
S  E  E  G  K  A  U  R  S  W  D  A  J  N  J
T  F  E  L  G  U  O  S  O  D  C  G  N  I  R
S  A  O  B  G  M  E  N  L  O  C  O  L  N  R
T  F  V  T  R  L  K  C  U  B  I  O  B  Y  C
H  S  W  E  R  A  Z  S  T  T  V  E  N  T  I
G  P  V  A  E  P  T  R  A  E  S  U  B  H  G
I  E  E  P  K  I  X  T  R  C  S  O  Z  G  W
N  F  S  J  C  P  U  D  A  N  K  X  N  I  B
D  F  F  W  U  P  U  X  G  I  Q  B  I  E  W
I  S  K  Y  E  P  L  Z  Z  X  P  P  R  C  N
M  Y  F  R  R  L  F  Z  B  K  C  N  C  W  G
```

Solution on page 113

Find these words...

LOVER	REPUTATION	FOLKLORE	MIDNIGHTS
FEARLESS	SPEAK NOW	EIGHTY-NINE	
EVERMORE	RED	ACOUSTIC	

Word search

Can you find these nine songs from
the Eras Tour set list?

```
T  M  E  V  C  G  Q  X  R  W  L  P  C  N  J
H  M  T  E  Z  W  X  M  O  L  D  D  L  N  J
G  Q  A  P  H  N  X  L  E  D  N  Q  E  F  Y
I  I  C  Z  O  C  L  W  W  Z  V  M  K  E  J
N  N  I  B  G  I  O  P  V  O  E  H  O  V  T
T  R  L  B  W  O  L  E  K  E  E  J  T  Q  N
R  F  E  Y  T  L  U  H  F  W  R  Y  U  N  Y
O  R  D  L  Y  R  O  T  S  E  V  O  L  T  F
F  O  L  P  V  X  M  G  U  T  M  D  P  G  J
K  A  I  K  T  U  L  N  Q  C  Y  Y  O  Z  N
O  J  M  L  O  L  F  F  P  A  D  L  V  I  W
R  T  Q  P  A  N  T  I  H  E  R  O  E  P  D
I  C  R  U  E  L  S  U  M  M  E  R  G  O  Q
Z  I  X  U  Q  Q  C  O  S  B  D  E  M  O  S
L  Y  P  F  D  E  T  N  A  H  C  N  E  I  P
```

Solution on page 113

Find these words...

CRUEL SUMMER	DELICATE	FORTNIGHT
LOVE STORY	ENCHANTED	STYLE
WILLOW	ALL TOO WELL	ANTI-HERO

Word search

Can you find these 10 supporting acts from the Eras Tour?

```
P  M  I  S  J  L  K  C  U  Z  B  X  K  T  J
H  D  C  U  M  A  U  J  N  P  H  A  I  M  O
O  E  E  S  B  A  X  V  R  K  O  C  I  Q  H
E  R  S  G  K  E  R  G  F  Q  Z  S  S  S  W
B  N  P  K  A  I  A  B  B  A  W  Z  O  K  X
E  I  I  L  B  Y  L  B  A  X  F  N  Q  X  N
B  L  C  I  P  L  L  G  A  E  Y  F  I  P  B
R  R  E  Q  A  K  B  E  Q  D  I  C  V  A  L
I  I  X  B  R  J  W  I  S  D  O  C  R  S  A
D  G  S  G  A  C  D  V  M  I  I  O  A  D  T
G  Y  A  T  M  S  V  K  V  N  Q  E  B  R  Z
E  C  T  F  O  E  Q  R  K  T  U  N  B  E  G
R  W  U  S  R  N  B  A  N  U  M  R  G  Z  E
S  J  O  M  E  V  J  E  R  F  W  J  R  C  J
E  W  L  X  Q  S  A  E  J  L  A  X  I  E  U
```

Solution on page 113

Find these words...

PARAMORE	BEABADOOBEE	LOUTA
PHOEBE BRIDGERS	GRACIE ABRAMS	ICE SPICE
HAIM	GIRL IN RED	
GAYLE	MUNA	

Quiz

Easy

1. In which American city did the Eras Tour begin?

_____

2. The Eras Tour is Taylor's ...
☐ Third
☐ Sixth
☐ Eighth
... concert tour.

3. How many acts are there in each Eras Tour show?

_____

4. Which is the first act?

_____

5. Which of Taylor's albums is not featured as one of the acts?

_____

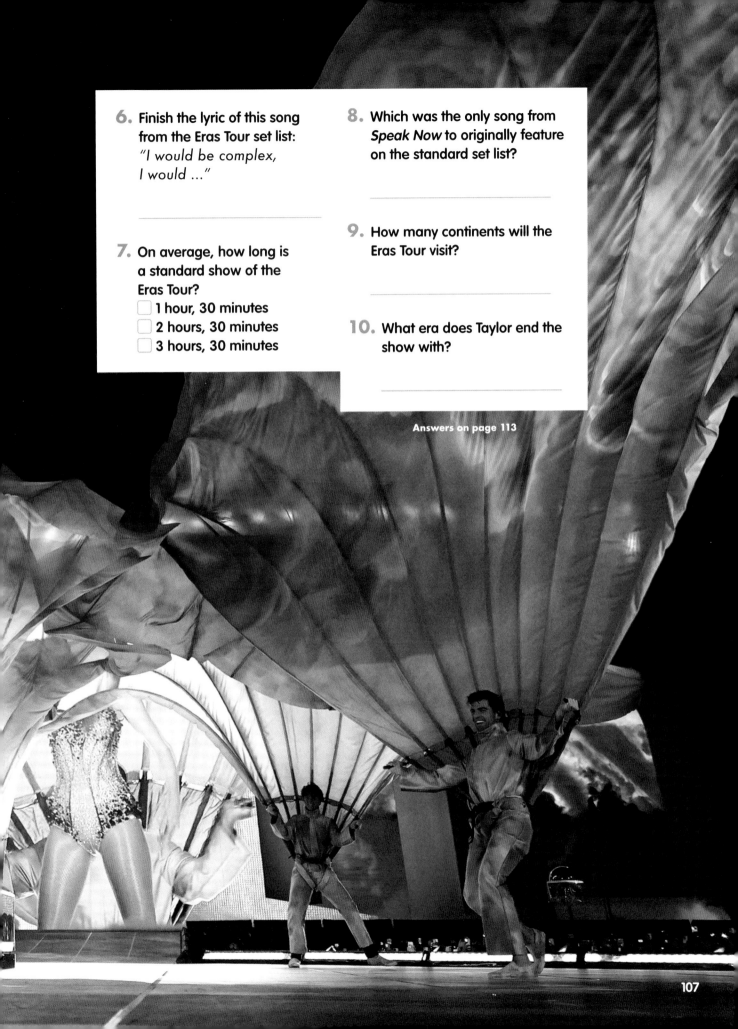

6. Finish the lyric of this song from the Eras Tour set list: *"I would be complex, I would ..."*

_____

7. On average, how long is a standard show of the Eras Tour?
- ☐ 1 hour, 30 minutes
- ☐ 2 hours, 30 minutes
- ☐ 3 hours, 30 minutes

8. Which was the only song from *Speak Now* to originally feature on the standard set list?

_____

9. How many continents will the Eras Tour visit?

_____

10. What era does Taylor end the show with?

_____

Answers on page 113

Quiz

Medium

1. What was the date of the opening Eras Tour show?

_____

2. Who were the opening acts of the tour's first night?

_____

3. How many tickets did Taylor sell on the opening day of the U.S. presale?
   ☐ 1.5 million
   ☐ 2.4 million
   ☐ 3.2 million

4. How many songs featured in the original standard set list?

_____

5. Which rapper joined Taylor onstage in East Rutherford?

6. Finish the lyric of this song from the Eras Tour set list: *"A friend to all is a friend to none, Chase two girls, ..."*

7. How many outfit changes has Taylor been known to perform in a night?

8. Which song does the Eras Tour close on?

9. In which city will the Eras Tour conclude in 2024?

10. True or False: The Eras Tour set list includes the 10-minute version of "All Too Well."

☐ True   ☐ False

Answers on page 113

Quiz

Hard

1. In which U.S. city did Swifties cause an earthquake during "Shake It Off"?

   _____

2. Who decorated Taylor's *Fearless* guitar for the tour?

   _____

3. The Eras Tour became the first concert tour to generate over ___ in revenue
   - [ ] $100 million
   - [ ] $1 billion
   - [ ] $10 billion

4. How many Guinness World Records did the Eras Tour achieve in 2023?

   _____

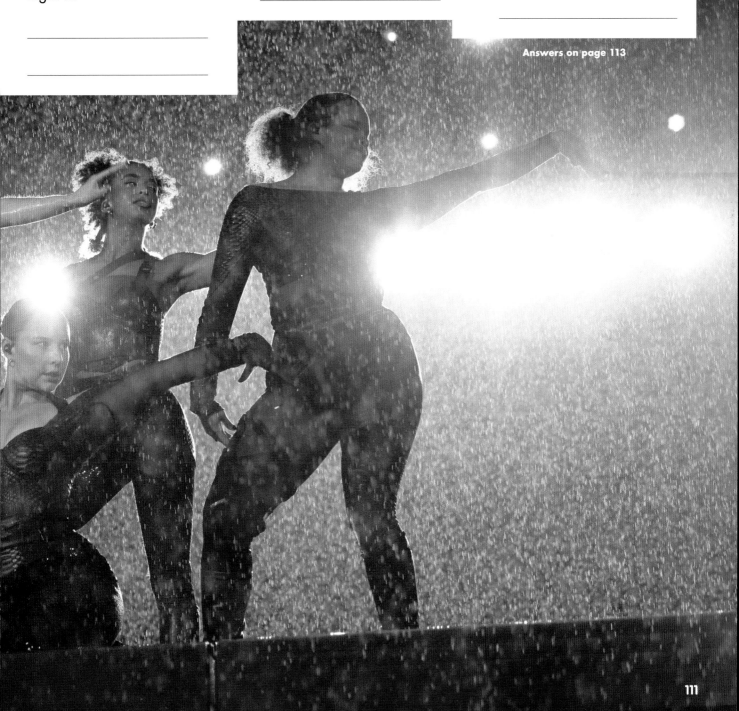

5. On which TV show did Taylor announce her Eras Tour?

_____

6. Finish the lyric of this song from the Eras Tour set list: *"You'll see me in hindsight Tangled up with you all night ..."*

_____

_____

7. Who directed the Eras Tour movie?

_____

8. What was the first surprise song to be repeated during the tour?

_____

9. How many shows did Taylor play during the U.S. leg of the tour in 2023?

_____

10. By the end of the tour, which venue will Taylor have performed at the most?

_____

Answers on page 113

Answers

Get Taylor to the stage

Spot the difference

Set list scramble

1. DELICATE
2. KARMA
3. LOVER
4. CARDIGAN
5. THE MAN
6. ENCHANTED

Word searches

Secret answer!

Eras Tour acts

```
D S R O U T T K E I T W E V Y
D E K D O O E R A S M O V I E
B S R P H U O T E E T N Q A P
Z X D L R L W X E V V W G E N
S E E G K A U R S W D A J N J
T F E L G U O S O D C G N I R
S A O B G M E N L O C O L N R
T F V T R L K C U B I O B Y C
H S W E R A Z S T T V E N T I
G P V A E P T R A E S U B H G
I E E P K I X T R C S O Z G W
N F S J C P U D A N K X N I B
D F F W U P U X G I Q B I E E
I S K Y E P L Z Z X P P R C N
M Y F R R L F Z B K C N C W G
```

Set list songs

```
T M E V C G Q X R W L P C N J
H M T E Z W X M O L D D L N J
G Q A P H N X L E D N Q E F Y
I I C Z O C L W W Z V M K E J
N N I B G I O P V O E H O V T
T R L B W O L E K E E J T Q N
R F E Y T L U H F W R Y U N Y
O R D L Y R O T S E V O L T F
F O L P V X M G U T M D P G J
K A I K T U L N Q C Y Y O Z N
O J M L O L F F P A D L V I W
R T Q P A N T I H E R O E P D
I C R U E L S U M M E R G O Q
Z I X U Q Q C O S B D E M O S
L Y P F D E T N A H C N E I P
```

Support acts

```
P M I S J L K C U Z B X K T J
H D C U M A U J N P H A I M O
O E E S B A X V R K O C I Q H
E R S G K E R G F Q Z S S S W
B N P K A I A B B A W Z O K X
E I I L B Y L B A X F N Q X N
B L C I P L L G A E Y F I P B
R R E Q A K B E Q D I C V A L
I I X B R J W I S D O C R S A
D G S G A C D V M I I O A D T
G Y A T M S V K V N Q E B R Z
E C T F O E Q R K T U N B E G
R W U S R N B A N U M R G Z E
S J O M E V J E R F W J R C J
E W L X Q S A E J L A X I E U
```

Quizzes

Easy

1. Glendale, Arizona
2. Sixth
3. 10
4. *Lover*
5. Her debut, *Taylor Swift*
6. "Be cool," from "The Man"
7. 3 hours, 30 minutes
8. "Enchanted"
9. 5
10. *Midnights*

Medium

1. March 17, 2023
2. Paramore and Gayle
3. 2.4 million
4. 44
5. Ice Spice
6. "Lose the one," from "cardigan"
7. Up to 16
8. "Karma"
9. Vancouver, Canada
10. True

Hard

1. Seattle
2. Her parents
3. $1 billion
4. 6
5. *Good Morning America*
6. "Burning it down," from "Wildest Dreams"
7. Sam Wrench
8. "Clean"
9. 53
10. Wembley, London (8 times)

Thunder Bay Press
An imprint of Printers Row Publishing Group
9717 Pacific Heights Blvd, San Diego, CA 92121
www.thunderbaybooks.com • mail@thunderbaybooks.com

Printers Row Publishing Group is a division of Readerlink Distribution Services, LLC.

Thunder Bay Press is a registered trademark of Readerlink Distribution Services, LLC.

Correspondence regarding the content of this book should be sent to Thunder Bay Press, Editorial Department, at the above address.

Thunder Bay Press
Publisher: Peter Norton
Associate Publisher: Ana Parker
Editor: Dan Mansfield

Future PLC
Editor: Dan Peel
Designer: Harriet Knight
Illustrator: Kym Winters

ISBN: 978-1-6672-0932-6
Printed in Beauceville, Canada
First printing, August 2024. TR/08/24
28 27 26 25 24   1 2 3 4 5

Image Credits
All imagery supplied by Getty Images
All copyrights and trademarks are recognized and respected